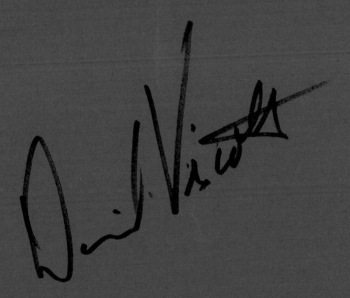

# What Every Kid Should Know

**BY JONAH KALB
AND DAVID VISCOTT, M.D.**

Houghton Mifflin
Company Boston

*Acknowledgments*

The illustrations that appear in the chapters
beginning on pages 52, 74, and 90 are by John Kuchera
and those in the chapters beginning on pages 10, 28,
and 108 are by Al Margolis. All artwork is reproduced
courtesy American Greetings Corporation, © 1974
American Greetings Corporation.

Library of Congress Cataloging in Publication Data

Kalb, Jonah.
    What every kid should know.

    SUMMARY: Discusses the problems of growing up and
gives suggestions on coping with various emotions,
understanding oneself, getting along with others, and
dealing with parents.
    1. Children—Conduct of life.      2. Youth—Conduct of
life.     |1. Conduct of Life|   I. Viscott, David S.,
1938-      joint author.   II. Title.
BJ1631.K3      170'.202'22      75-45123
ISBN 0-395-24386-6

PRINTED IN THE UNITED STATES OF AMERICA.

v  10  9  8  7  6  5  4

For Laura, Eugene, Liz, Penny, Jon,
Melanie and Aimee

# TABLE OF CONTENTS

# INTRODUCTION

Growing up — being the kid you want to be now, and becoming the adult you want to become later — is very difficult. A lot of things, and a lot of people, are in the way.

The biggest roadblock, however, is not knowing that *everybody* has a hard time growing up, that *everybody* has feelings that are difficult to understand and deal with, that *everybody* has problems with his parents, that *everybody* needs friends. Every kid is occasionally lonely, every kid is unsure of himself, every kid puts himself down.

This book has two purposes. First, by writing it down and putting it in print, maybe you will begin to believe that you are not the only one with these problems. Maybe you will begin to believe that you are really okay after all.

The second purpose is to explain things, so that you will understand them. Understanding feelings, relationships, and attitudes is the first step in dealing with them.

Kids are not "little adults." Kids are "becoming adults," and there is a big difference. We hope this book will help you "become."

So many kids these days have parents who are divorced, or getting divorced, that there is a special chapter on that subject in the back of the book. Kids of divorcing parents have some special added problems, but understanding is still the first step in dealing with them.

If your parents are not divorcing, you should probably read the chapter anyway, so that you can understand what some of your friends are going through.

# ABOUT
# FEELINGS

Everyone has feelings, even if he can't always describe them accurately. Anger is a feeling. So is joy. So is sadness. So is fear.

There are many words that describe feelings.

Irritation, anger, and rage are not different emotions. They are different degrees of the same feeling — anger. Displeasure, sadness, and depression are also degrees of the same feeling — sadness.

Basically, there are two kinds of feelings.

The first kind make you feel good. They are feelings of joy, happiness, love. They are feelings of affection, caring, and contentment.

The other kind of feelings make you uncomfortable. They are feelings of hurt, fear, anger, guilt, inadequacy, depression, envy, jealousy, and hate.

And then there are also mixed feelings, where two or more opposite feelings about the same person or event are present at the same time. When people have mixed feelings, they are confused, and often don't know how to act.

Your feelings influence how you think and reason. And they influence your adjustment to everyone and everything around you.

Feelings are very, very important.

## What Do Feelings Tell You?

The *kind* of feeling you have tells you your true emotional reaction to everything you experience. And so, it really tells you a lot about yourself.

The *strength* of the feeling is like a thermometer. It tells you how important the feeling is. That, too, tells you a lot about yourself.

If you spend time with a friend joking and having fun, your feelings are telling you that you like being with your friend. These positive feelings make you see the world in a happy way.

But if you go to a party everyone seems to be enjoying but you are feeling sad, your feelings are trying to tell you something. Perhaps you are displeased with yourself. They may be reminding you that you miss someone's company. You may be feeling left out. You may wish you could give a party as nice.

Or you may feel guilty for being there when you really should be home studying. The sad feeling could be telling you any number of things.

# Some Feelings Hang Around

Uncomfortable feelings often seem to hang around for a long time. Often when you're sad, you feel sad much longer than the event seems to deserve. It certainly would be more convenient for everyone if we could control feelings and send them away. If something upsets us at ten in the morning and we could feel better by eleven, that would be just fine.

But feelings don't seem to work like that. Feelings have to run their natural course and that takes emotional energy. People have only a limited amount of emotional energy.

There are, however, certain things that can be done — things that speed uncomfortable feelings along their way.

The best way to get rid of uncomfortable feelings is to analyze and understand them. Then, in some cases, you might be able to do something more to settle them. But even if there is nothing more that you can do, just the understanding will help.

# How to Analyze Your Feelings

Everybody wants to be happy — to experience joy, contentment, love, affection, and all the other good feelings. That is one of the objectives of a good, rich life.

Happy feelings don't really need to be analyzed. Just enjoy them.

But uncomfortable feelings do need analysis because they stand in the way of the happy feelings. They prevent you from feeling good by draining your energy.

This chapter is meant to be used as a guide, to help you understand what certain uncomfortable feelings are, and where they come from. It should help you analyze why you feel a certain way, and it should help you decide what you can do about it.

To start with, sit down in some quiet place where you can think. Then, try to match how you feel with the different feelings described in the next pages.

## Hurt

You feel hurt when you lose something. But it's sometimes difficult to know what it is that you have lost.

You feel hurt when someone criticizes you, because you may have lost some of your own self-esteem.

You feel hurt when a friend criticizes you, because you value his opinion of you and hate to lose his positive feelings toward you.

You also feel hurt when you lose a friendship and all the good feelings in that friendship.

You may begin to feel bad about yourself because you may think you're not likable any more.

Any important loss can especially hurt you if the loss makes you feel worth less.

If you feel hurt, try to find out what you have lost. Is it a friend, or a possession, or a good opinion of yourself? Ask why that loss was important to you. What did the friend mean to you? Why was the possession important?

Often, people you know very well and like very much can hurt you more than strangers because they are more important to you. When they hurt you, it *really* hurts.

# Fear

Fear is worrying about being hurt or about losing something very important to you.

You can fear a physical hurt — such as being afraid of dark alleys because you think someone might beat you up. Or you can fear the loss of self-worth resulting from, let's say, flunking a test.

Fear has an important purpose. It prepares a person for possible danger by causing the body to release chemicals into the bloodstream. These chemicals make the person alert and prepared to defend himself.

Being nervous is a form of fear. Another name for fear is "being anxious." A kid who is unprepared in school might be anxious that the teacher will call on him; he fears a loss of self-esteem by being shown up.

If you feel afraid, consider what it is you fear losing or how you could be hurt. After you think it over, you may decide that your fears are exaggerated. If so, you'll be able to continue with a clear mind.

Of course, you may decide that a serious threat really does exist and that you have good reason to be afraid. You'd better reconsider what you're doing and make sure you're prepared. You'll never know unless you think it through.

Do something about your fears if you can. If you fear losing your bicycle when you leave it unlocked, go back and lock it. If you're worried about your dog getting hit by a car, tie him up.

But at least find out what you're afraid of. Unknown fears become exaggerated and drain your energy.

Everyone feels fear some of the time. There is no such thing as a fearless person. However, everyone fears something different. Each person fears losing something important to him. And people value things differently. A football player doesn't usually worry about hurting his fingers. A pianist, however, does.

As kids grow older, their childhood fears go away. Few adults are fearful of the dark, of dogs, or of loud noises, although many kids are.

Some fears can become larger than they need to be. A kid who was once bitten by a dog may fear all dogs. His fear may make him avoid streets where dogs live, perhaps even all the streets where he *thinks* dogs *might* live. A fear like this has grown way out of proportion; it can make the kid more concerned with avoiding dogs than with living.

Most unreasonable fears like this can be overcome. Instead of avoiding dogs, it is possible to take a new look at dogs and learn that all dogs do not bite and that most dogs can be friends.

A new look, from time to time, at an unreasonable fear is worth trying.

No one should force you to do something that you fear, but you shouldn't avoid something just because you feel *some* fear about it. Everyone fears new things — like going to a new school, or going to camp, or taking part in a new sport, or learning to swim, or riding a horse for the first time. It's only natural because you don't know what to expect, and everyone fears the unknown. But if you let your anxieties over these new adventures prevent you from trying them, you will be missing a great deal in your life.

The way to conquer your fears begins with admitting to yourself that you're afraid. Being afraid means you're only being human, not weak. Admitting you are afraid is a sign of strength. Then decide just what it is you are afraid of — what it is you think you might lose. And then take steps to prepare yourself, if you can, so you don't lose it. That means knowing your weak points and taking them into consideration.

# Anger

Everybody gets angry some of the time, and they usually get angry over hurt.

If someone tells you that he never gets angry, he's either mistaken or fooling himself.

How angry you get depends both upon how hurt you are and how you let your hurt and angry feelings out. If you keep these feelings inside, anger will build up.

You can expect to be angry at a teacher who criticizes you in front of the whole class. Or at a friend who no longer wants to be your friend. Or at a parent who punishes you, especially if you don't think you deserve it. You can expect to be angry at people who cheat you and who make fun of you — in fact, at anyone who hurts you.

Anger comes from hurt. And hurt, you remember, comes from loss.

It's important to make sure that angry feelings are expressed. Angry feelings should not be held in and allowed to grow because anger has a way of taking over control of other feelings.

Unexpressed anger can occupy all your thoughts,

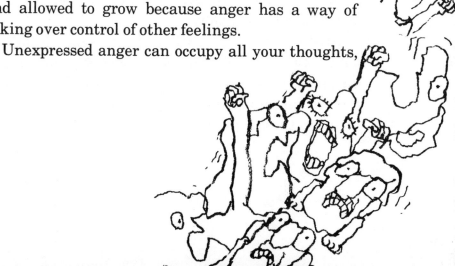

or it can cause you to get angry in the wrong place. So you have to deal with your anger at its source — at the hurt feelings. It may not be easy to tell a friend that he hurt you, but it's better to do that than to have unexpressed angry feelings about him that could ruin the friendship.

## Guilt from Anger

When anger isn't expressed, it often becomes directed toward the person who feels it and is then called guilt. When a person feels guilty, he feels unworthy and "to blame" for everything.

People often feel guilty because they have done something that they feel they should not have done. Often, there is a good deal of fear along with this guilt — a fear of being found out. A boy who breaks a window with his sling shot, for example, is both afraid of being discovered and guilt-ridden for having broken the window.

Another source of guilt feelings comes from letting someone down. Young people try to meet standards of behavior and performance set by adults. School, parents, and friends have expectations. Frequently, these expectations are impossible to meet.

When someone knows he has disappointed others, he becomes disappointed and angry with himself and with the people he disappoints. Guilt often results.

Still, most guilt feelings come from unexpressed anger at other people, which cannot be released and is eventually directed at yourself. This is how it works:

Suppose your mother hurts you and makes you angry. Because you think it may be wrong to be angry with a person you love or respect like your mother, you may have mixed feelings of love and anger and be unable to express that anger. You may convince yourself that the trouble is really with you. Or you may not be able to express the anger for fear of the consequences. If you express anger at your mother, you may fear that she may be hurt, and get angry at you.

Whatever the reason for not expressing anger, it is eventually directed at yourself. The anger builds and so does the guilt. More angry thoughts lead to more guilt.

And you may think of yourself as an evil person to have such angry thoughts.

Guilt can do very strange and upsetting things to people — especially young people who have less experience. If you feel guilty enough, for example, you may try to get yourself punished. Some young people feel so much guilt that they get into trouble just to get themselves caught by the police.

They want someone to punish them. Sound unbelievable? It happens every day.

When a person feels guilty there's a lot he can do to feel better. If you've hurt someone, you could apologize, in the hope that the other person will forgive you and reassure you that you are really okay. You could also express your anger. If you express the anger at the proper person, the anger is let out and the guilt will decrease. If someone hurts you, tell him so. No matter how angry you are, don't lose your temper. It will only make you feel worse. Learn to tell people when they hurt you and don't waste time putting it off.

And finally, when you're angry, say to the person you're angry with, "I'm angry with you," just like that, and tell them why. Very often you'll find that your anger is justified. You'll clear the air and feel better.

# Depression

If feelings of guilt grow and are not settled, they can lead to strong feelings of sadness called depression. When people get depressed they feel guilty, angry, hurt, and are often unable to express it. Fortunately, although young people often feel sad, they seldom feel so sad that they can be called depressed.

When people are very depressed, they frequently cannot eat. They often get sloppy, walk around feeling very bad, cannot concentrate on their jobs or on their schoolwork, have trouble with their sleeping habits, and don't enjoy anything. Mostly, they feel terrible about themselves.

All people are sad now and then, but mostly for short periods of time. If a depression lasts for very long, or is repeated again and again, one right after another, it is probably a good idea to talk it over with a doctor. But feeling sad once in a while is human and perfectly normal.

Many mistakes are cured with time, but some just don't go away. If you feel depressed, it is worth looking at your whole situation carefully, talking it over with an adult, and seeing if there is something you can do to solve the problem.

# Envy

Feelings of envy are wishes to have what the other person has, or to be like the other person. They indicate that you have some dissatisfaction about the way you are yourself.

If you are envious, you are dissatisfied with yourself in some *important* way.

Feelings of envy do not need expression. They need you to understand them and then to do something about the shortcomings you see in yourself. If you can't do anything about them, you must learn to accept yourself the way you are.

If you are envious of someone's good grades in school, you do not have to express these feelings. What would be a better idea is to study harder and improve your own grades.

Often, if you examine the cause of your envy, you'll discover that you do not *really* want what the other person has. What you really want is to be better yourself. And you can have that if you work at it. When a person does what he loves and does it well, he seldom feels envious of anyone.

# Jealousy

Jealousy is the wish that someone had positive feelings toward you *instead* of toward someone else. Feelings of jealousy almost always come from feeling insecure about yourself, and believing that other people are better than you are.

Jealous feelings are most commonly seen when one person likes someone who likes someone else even better. Jealousy is a painful and destructive feeling. It causes hurt and anger to everyone involved. To overcome feelings of jealousy, you have to learn to like yourself better.

When you like yourself better, you can accept the idea that everyone is free to like and love whomever they choose, and that just because somebody likes somebody else more, that doesn't mean that you are unlikable, or that no one will ever like you best.

# Loneliness

Everyone feels lonely some of the time. Loneliness is a feeling just like anger, and sadness, and joy. But some people feel that they are lonely because there is something the matter with them.

Young people especially have trouble measuring themselves against suitable standards in any case. The standards and ideals they set for themselves only yesterday may seem out of place today. And the standards their parents and teachers set for them may be very far off base. Kids live in their own rapidly changing world, and their views of themselves keep changing along with everything else.

When people feel lonely, they often attack themselves. They may conclude that they are lonely because they are unlovable. They think they're without friends because they are not worthy of friends. They feel unliked because they think of themselves as unlikable.

None of this is probably true. But in the quiet of his own thoughts, each person must understand that everyone is lonely sometimes, and he must try to accept what he can't change and do his best to improve what he can.

# Why Get Involved?

You may have read this chapter and decided that, with all the troubles feelings can create, the best thing to do is to limit your feelings by limiting your involvement with others. It's true that if you don't care about anything or anybody, losing them will not hurt you, and also you won't get angry, or feel guilty, or get depressed.

But if you do not get involved, you cannot share joy, or happiness, or love, or contentment either. And you sure are going to be very lonely.

The price you pay for loving is that you will miss that special person when he is not around.

The price you pay for a friendship is that you risk losing it.

In life, the price you pay for maybe winning is the risk you take in maybe losing.

Emotions are part of life and you cannot avoid them. The important thing is to understand your feelings, know what they are, and know how to deal with them. In the end, it's the only way to be happy.

# ABOUT
# DEALING
# WITH
# PARENTS

Sooner or later, every kid has problems with his parents. Even kids who think they get along very well with their parents have problems with their parents. Problems between kids and parents are only normal and natural.

There are several reasons for this.

For one thing, one of the ways a person learns about himself and about the world around him is by testing and pushing his parents to their limits. Testing and pushing parents, however, eventually leads to conflict.

When someone reaches his teens, he is exposed to a great many ideas that did not originate in his own home. If he adopts some of these ideas, it will often lead to conflict with his parents. This is normal because parents, like anyone else, like things to go their way.

Growing children also learn, much to their surprise, that their parents are not perfect. When children are very young, they often don't know this. When a kid discovers that his parents don't know everything and can't do everything, his disappointment often leads to conflict, especially if he looks to others for leadership whose advice goes against his parent's attitudes.

Also, there really is a generation gap. Things that were right for your parents when they were kids may not be right for you — and it's sometimes hard for parents to understand that. This difference also leads to conflict.

Then, too, many parents are rigid and unreasonable — which leads to conflict.

And many kids are rigid and unreasonable — which also leads to conflict.

Not all conflict between parents and children is bad. After all, kids really do need to grow up, they do need to test their ideas, and they do need to try out values other than the ones they learn about at home. Such conflict often leads to new understanding on both sides and is good.

There is another, less helpful kind of conflict in families. Sometimes parents and kids argue and fight so much that they expect that *all* of their rela-

tionship will be in conflict. Even reasonable requests by one party are *automatically* met with resistance by the other. Nobody examines the problem from the other's point of view. That is bad conflict because it leads only to more conflict and no growth.

## Rights

And also, there is a great deal of conflict between children and parents based on misunderstanding each other's rights. When children don't know what they're entitled to, they fight for everything.

One way to look at this "bad" conflict and resolve it satisfactorily is to clearly spell out certain "rights" that all children have, certain other "rights" that all parents have, and certain areas of the relationship where nobody has "rights." Decisions in this last area should be the subject for bargaining, in which each side gives in a little.

Rights vary from family to family, but this chapter is about "rights" which apply to most families. If you're having trouble with your parents, it might be wise to try to seek agreement on "rights." Just learning who has what rights will clear up a lot of misunderstanding.

# Rights Carry Responsibilities

Rights are not absolute. Just because Freedom of Speech is guaranteed by the Constitution does not mean that you can stand up in a movie theater and yell "Fire!"

So no rights are unlimited and all rights must be used with responsibility, especially in your family. If you use your rights with restraint and intelligence, you can expect to keep them. If you use your rights dangerously, or without regard to the rights of others, you can expect to lose them simply because someone will take them away from you. If you have a right such as the use of your bicycle, you have to use it with reasonable care without endangering others.

# A Bill of Rights for Kids

## You Have a Right to Pick Your Own Friends

Kids have friends for reasons that are often not clear to anyone, except to themselves and their friends, and sometimes not even to them. Parents often have strong opinions about who should be their kids' friends. Sometimes parents try to force a friendship between two kids who don't like each other. And more often parents try to break up friendships they think unsuitable.

Some parents want their children to make friends only with good students, hoping that they will pick up some "brains," or at least good study habits. Many parents insist that their kids make friends only with "nice" boys and girls because parents fear their child's friend will get him into trouble with the law or with school. Some parents want their children to have only polite, well-mannered friends, even though their own kids find them dull.

Within limits, you have the right to pick your own friends and to be with the kids you like.

What are these limits? If a friend does lead you into trouble, then it is at least partly *your* fault for associating with him. Your parents have the right to see that it doesn't happen again. If you choose to hang around with people who can lead you into trouble, that is your right. But if you get into trouble, you can expect to lose that right. You see, your responsibility is to stay out of trouble. If you can't stay out of trouble by yourself, it's your parents' responsibility to help.

In short, the right to pick your own friends is yours, so long as you show the responsibility that goes with it.

# You Have a Right to an Explanation

You don't have to take "no" for a complete answer. You are entitled to an explanation.

Many times, your parents say "no" without really thinking it through, and asking them to "explain" might even get them to change their minds. Your parents may behave the way they do toward you because that's the way that *their* parents acted toward them. If you can get them to explain their reasons, it sometimes becomes obvious to them that times have changed, and they might be more willing to compromise or change their ideas.

How do you get an explanation? First, stay *calm*. Tell your parents you understand they have refused your request and you will follow their decision, but you want to understand better why they said "no" and what their thinking was. If you don't agree with them, and you remain calm, you can usually make your own points understood. They may even see your side.

Sometimes your parents will be right in saying "no." You have a responsibility to listen and consider what they say. And sometimes, you might just have to take "no" for an answer. But get an explanation first. The point is that you need the chance to discuss both sides.

# You Have a Right to Be Yourself

You have an absolute right — to become the person you really are.

Many parents, unfortunately, have very specific ideas about what they would like their children to be when they grow up — and they spend a great deal of time and effort trying to mold their kid in that idea. Some parents want their sons or their daughters to be doctors or lawyers. And any time their kid wants to do something else, something *he* or *she* wants, there are conflicts.

When a parent feels strongly about what his child should become, he may be trying to relive his own life through his child or trying to justify his own life to himself. Although this is your parent's problem, it will become yours unless you stick up for your own right to be yourself — to be just the kind of person you really are and, eventually, to become the kind of adult you yourself want to be.

BUT, in being yourself, there are limits. Being yourself is not permission to interfere with other people's rights.

# You Have a Right to Privacy

You have a right to keep secrets. You have the right to have telephone conversations in private. You have the right to sit in your room, with your own thoughts, without interruption.

It is important to be alone once in a while. Growing up is not easy. It often takes time to consider all your choices and to get a good perspective on what is happening to you. Being alone allows you to look at both your good and your bad points without worrying what other people think.

Remember that other people also have the right to privacy, and you must respect that right.

The right to privacy does not mean that you can lie. You still have to own up to doing something like breaking a vase. The right to privacy is not a right to be dishonest. And your right to privacy does not mean that you may withdraw from the family whenever you want to.

## You Have a Right to Property

Even though you did not pay for most of the possessions you have, you own them. They are yours and nobody should be able to take them away from you without good reasons, reasons which should be understood by both parties before something is taken away.

Unless you feel you own your possessions, it is difficult to learn to care for them and develop a pride of ownership or a sense of responsibility.

Since your property is yours, you have the right to

lend it to other people, you have the right to trade it away for something else, and you have the right to lose it, break it, or spoil it. You have the right to say who may, and who may not, use it. All within reason.

BUT, there are responsibilities. If you lose or break something through carelessness, you have no right to expect your parents to replace it. If you lend it, you do so on your own responsibility, and if it doesn't come back, that is no concern of your parents (although they might help you get it back). If you trade your bike for a ball, though, your parents will probably have something to say about your judgment.

When your parents restrict your use of a possession, it is not the same as taking it away. If you ride your bicycle dangerously, your parents may say that you cannot use it for a week. If you abuse your property, your parents may properly restrict your use of it for a period of time, so long as you get it back eventually. Actually, they're doing you a favor, if you think about it, because they're showing you that they care.

Remember, other people have the same property rights as you. If you take your sister's things without permission, you may expect her to take yours. If you want your own property rights respected, you have to respect other people's.

# You Have a Right to Your Own Opinion

Even though your parents or friends might not agree with you, you have a right to your own opinion. It is all right to disagree with your parents. It is all right to disagree with anybody. Nobody can tell you what to think.

Whether you *express* your opinion or not is another matter. In a family meeting where vacations are being discussed, or in a school debate, everybody expects you to express your opinion. But if you think your parents are old-fashioned, making a big point of it in a loud voice in the middle of a restaurant is not such a good idea. That's not free speech; it's blowing up to embarrass someone.

Whether, when, and how to express your opinion is a matter of judgment. A good rule is to avoid hurting other people's feelings. If you avoid hurting people, you can usually express your opinion freely.

# You Have the Right to Be Taken Seriously

Not only have you the right to an opinion, but you have the right to have that opinion taken seriously. There is nothing so annoying as being ignored. You are a person, just as everyone else in your family is a person, and you have the right to be treated as a person.

You have a right to be taken seriously, especially when you are frightened. Then everything around you seems threatening. You really need to be listened to by your parents.

Some things are very important to kids that are not really important to their parents. Losing a game might be crucial to you, but not to your parents. You have a right to make them understand why something is important to you.

But there are limits to this too. You may be getting upset about something that, in the long run, really does not matter too much, and your parents may help to show you that. If you are silly about everything all of the time, your parents cannot take you seriously at all. So don't demand to be taken seriously unless you really mean it.

# You Have a Right to Your Own Thoughts

Most kids have some thoughts that they find upsetting, such as angry thoughts or sexual thoughts. Young people worry about their thoughts and ideas and often wonder if they are crazy for having them. There is no thought that you can have, no matter how weird, embarrassing, or upsetting, that someone else hasn't already had. Almost everybody has had the same upsetting thoughts at one time in their lives. No thoughts, by themselves, are evil or bad. Your private thoughts are your own private bus·ness.

But there is a big difference between thinking something and doing it. Although you have the right to think what you like, you are responsible for your actions. You can *feel* like hurting your brother or sister, for example, but that doesn't mean you *can* hurt them.

## You Have the Right to Feel the Way You Do

You have the right to feel happy and joyous, sad, angry, anxious, or anything else you want. They are your feelings and you're entitled to them.

Your feelings are your true reactions to the world around you and are important in your development as a person — maybe more important than almost anything else. Knowing what you feel and why you feel that way is important in learning to adjust to life.

BUT you cannot impose your feelings on other people who do not feel the same way. If you are sad and angry, and you are invited to a party, you do not have the right to go and spoil the party for everyone else.

## You Have a Right to Have Your Parents Spend Time with You

Some parents spend very little time with their kids. They usually don't mean this as punishment. And it isn't because they don't like their kids. But parents do get tied up in their own world with busi-

ness, with friends, and with chores; and they sometimes forget to set aside time to spend with their
kids.

If you are in a situation like that, you can do something about it. Ask your parents when it would be a
good time for them to sit down with you to talk.
Very few parents would refuse to do that. When
you do talk to them, say very simply and pleasantly
that you would like to spend more time with them,
and ask them to set aside some time each week for
doing something together.

Sometimes this is difficult for a parent to do, especially in large families.

Most parents who don't spend enough time with
their kids simply do not realize it. When it is called
to their attention, they almost always correct the
situation. If you feel this way, there is no better way
to solve the problem than by talking to them about
it.

# You Have a Right to Money of Your Own

You have the right to your own money.

Kids usually get money by earning it, by receiving it as gifts, or by getting an allowance from their parents.

Usually, part of that allowance is "free" money, and you should be free to spend that part any way you like. Some part of that allowance is usually "restricted" money, to be set aside for school lunches, bus fares, school supplies, and so forth.

Money that you earn yourself is another story. Usually, if you save for something, you should be allowed to buy it. The spending of large amounts of money that you may have received as gifts should be with your parents' advice and consent. It is still your money and should be spent *for* you, but it shouldn't be wasted. How you spend large amounts of money often depends upon your age and your family's needs.

The way to learn how to handle money is to manage some of your own money yourself. You may want to ask your parents' advice, but the final decision should be yours. You may spend some of it unwisely; that is part of the learning process. It's better to misuse a little money now than not know how to manage a lot of money later.

# You Have the Right to Your Own Taste

You should be allowed to decorate your room however you like providing you don't destroy it. Within reason and the current standards of your age group, you should be able to select your own clothes and choose your own hairstyle. You have the right to listen to music you like and to watch the kind of television shows that you like, but not necessarily as loud or as often as you'd like. That may be interfering with other people's rights. In general, you have the right to your own taste in everything.

Standards of style among kids are important. If your group wears long hair, you might feel left out if you wear short hair. If all your friends wear jeans or corduroys, and you don't, again you will feel left out. It's important to be accepted by your friends.

Unfortunately, many parents do not understand or accept this, even though they dress in a style that makes them acceptable to their groups.

Sometimes parents get upset over their children's taste because they're afraid of losing control over them. Try to understand their feelings and discuss your disagreements together, patiently, calmly, and slowly. Perhaps you may have to win one point at a time.

# Parents Have Rights, Too

Your parents have rights, too. And like your rights, theirs involve limits and responsibilities.

If you do not respect your parents' rights, there is no reason for you to expect them to respect yours.

In general, parents have the following rights: to be themselves, to pick their own friends, to feel the way they do, and to be taken seriously. They are also entitled to time with their kids, money and tastes of their own, privacy, property, and their own opinions and thoughts.

Children violate their parents' rights as often as parents violate theirs. Many parents are just not taken seriously by their kids. Many children attack their parents' taste. Many think it unnecessary to give an explanation for their behavior. Many spend practically no time at home at all, except to eat and sleep. Think about it. It's a two-way street.

But in addition to these, parents have other rights, too.

## Parents Have the Right to Be Treated as People

Every parent has the right to be treated as a person by his own child, which means being treated with the same respect any other adult deserves.

You wouldn't walk into your classroom and yell at your teacher and demand that your teacher bring you a piece of paper. You don't treat any other adult as a personal servant, and you shouldn't treat your mother and father that way.

True, some parents do yell at their children and order them around. It is unfortunate, and they are wrong. They should be setting the right example. If they fail in this respect, *you* have to set the example.

Treat your parents with courtesy and respect, even if they sometimes don't deserve it. You'll discover that they'll soon treat you the same way.

## Parents Have the Right to Set Limits

Parents have the right to decide how much is "enough," and when a time is "too late." You can discuss this with them, but the final decision is theirs to make: what time you must be home, how much allowance you should get, how long you can talk on the telephone, and, generally, what time you must go to bed. Parents can determine which behavior is "not all right." You may believe that they are wrong and unfair. If so, tell them what you think.

Parents are responsible for your safety and welfare, and they have the right to make rules to protect you even if you do not always agree with those rules. Again, they should always be open to discussion, but the final decision is theirs.

## Parents Have the Right to Enforce Their Rules

Breaking rules or violating the rights of others may call for punishment, and parents have the right to set that punishment. That, too, should be discussed and the punishment should be fair, but the right to set punishment still belongs to your parents.

The best punishment is one that fits the "crime." If you misuse your bicycle, your punishment should be loss of the bicycle for a period of time. But you shouldn't lose the bicycle for a month just for leaving it in the rain.

## Parents Have the Right to Make Suggestions

Even though there are many times in your life when you must decide what to do, your parents shouldn't feel that they must remain silent when they think you are making a mistake.

For example, you may want to misuse something valuable. Your parents should be free to tell you so.

Your parents are your most important advisors since most parents really do have the best interests of their children at heart. They may not always be right, and you may not always agree with them; but they *do* have the right to make suggestions, and you *do* have the obligation to take them seriously.

# Working It Out

If you feel your rights are being violated, sit down with your parents and talk about it. If you keep your temper and discuss things calmly, there's a good chance that your rights will be appreciated and restored.

Most conflicts in a family can be worked out by open and honest discussion, using this chapter as a guide to each other's rights.

If your parents find it difficult to accept the fact that you are growing up or have rights, keep discussing the problem with them. Don't give up. Sooner or later, they will have to accept the fact that you are mature enough to make up your own mind.

Dealing with parents is not really that much different from dealing with other people. Remember respect, courtesy, and mutual rights.

# ABOUT
# DEALING
# WITH
# FRIENDS

Everybody needs friends, but nobody needs friends more than young people do. Growing up is complicated and confusing.

Young people are often unsure of themselves. They doubt their actions. They often say things they don't mean. They often wonder whether they are doing the right thing, or following the right goals, or behaving in the right way. They often wonder if they are being phony.

Because all young people feel this way at one time or another, it is important for them to be able to check things out with others in the same situation — with friends.

Adults will sometimes talk over problems with a kid and sometimes parents will. But when a youngster talks with an adult, they are often talking on two different levels. Although adults may know more, kids have more in common with other kids. Kids look at events from the same viewpoint, share the same problems, the same frustrations, and the same fears. As a result, only a kid can really give another kid the reassurance and the acceptance that really matter most.

If you're worried about flunking a test, only someone with similar worries can really understand how you feel. If you're worried about being popular, only someone who is also worried about being popular can reassure you. No matter how much your mother likes you, she can't take the place of a best friend your own age.

Without friends, people often grow up feeling left out and spend their lives wondering if something is wrong with them. Often, they become adults who feel they don't belong.

## What Is a Friend?

In a sense, everybody already knows what a friend is. But when you try to define friendship, it gets complicated. Still, it is important to put down ideas about what a friend is so that you know what to expect and what to value.

Here are some ideas:

A friend is someone who shares the same interests

as you and who has many of the same opinions and attitudes.

A friend is someone who trusts you, and understands you, and accepts you the way you are. He is someone whom you trust, understand, and accept in return.

A friend is someone who shares some of the viewpoints you consider important.

A friend will not attack you where you can really be hurt because friends are vulnerable in the same way. A true friend already knows how you feel about certain things without having to be told. He knows how bad you feel because he's hurt the same way.

A friend is someone who knows that you are only human, and he takes that into consideration in dealing with you. He doesn't expect you to be perfect. You do the same for him.

A friend is someone who knows what is really important to you, because you have felt close enough to him in the past to share your feelings, dreams, and plans with him.

## How Do Friendships Grow?

Friendships generally begin with acquaintances — people to whom you say "hi," or kids you meet fairly often at meetings of a stamp club, or neighborhood kids with whom you play sports, or sing, or something like that.

A friendship develops from an acquaintance when there is sharing, especially sharing of important things like feelings and hopes. Sharing doesn't usually develop until two people begin to trust each other. Nobody shares anything important with just anyone. Trust grows from understanding. Usually you must know a person pretty well before you can

really trust him. When you trust someone, you believe he won't hurt you.

That means there is work involved in developing and maintaining a friendship. It begins with getting to know somebody as well as you can. Then when you understand that person, you begin trusting and sharing, and soon a friendship begins.

It's not always simple for an acquaintance to grow — from knowing, to trusting, to sharing — into a good and lasting friendship, however. All friendships, even the best, have their ups and downs, their fights, squabbles, misunderstandings, and reconciliations. Just because things aren't always going right between you and a friend, it doesn't mean the friendship is ended.

Everyone grows and changes, especially young people. And as they grow, so do their interests and attitudes. What you may believe with all your heart today, you may think is silly next year. As you change, and your friends change, so your friendships change too. Sometimes you may outgrow your friends, and sometimes they may outgrow you. If you lose a friendship this way, no one is at fault. You should be careful not to blame anyone for growing up or for changing, including yourself.

# How to Make Friends

No book can tell you exactly what to do to make friends. There just isn't any magic formula. But there are some tips that might help. Here are a few positive things to do:

*If you're new in the neighborhood.* Let's suppose you just moved to a new neighborhood where you don't know anyone. The best way to make friends is to follow your old interests. If you were a stamp collector in your old neighborhood, join a stamp club. If you were an athlete in the old neighborhood, try out for some teams. If you were a singer, join a chorus. In that way, you already find a collection of people with at least one common interest to build upon, and you'll be having a good time. It is easier to be attractive to others when you're having a good time.

*If you have no special interests.* It sometimes happens, though not as often as you might think, that a person isn't especially good at anything, doesn't have any special interests, or doesn't follow a particular hobby. If you're like that, you might join some general organizations that will help you develop special interests. Scouts, for example, often introduces a kid to a whole range of new interests he might like. Church groups and school clubs also often introduce kids to special activities that remain with them for the rest of their lives. Just don't sit back doing nothing besides complaining that you have no friends.

*Be yourself.* This is a good rule, not only for making friends, but for keeping them as well. A friendship must be honest if it is going to last. You wouldn't want to make friends with someone because he believed a lie you told him, or because you pretended to be someone you really weren't. You want friends to accept you the way you really are, and therefore you'd do best to act the way you really are.

*Be willing to try new things.* A lot of kids decide that they don't like something before they really try it. They are afraid to fail or to look foolish. Nobody expects you to be good at everything. So if you don't try something new, you'll never know if you like it. What's worse, you might miss out on the friends that might come with that new interest.

*Join group activities.* Some kinds of activities are better than others for making friends. In sports, basketball and baseball are better than weightlifting or some other individual sport. Trying out for the school play is another good group activity. In a group activity, someone else *depends* on you. You matter. Without your contribution, the play or team or choral group would not be the same. Such groups often lead to good friendships, because depending on you leads to a certain bond of trust. And trust, you remember, is important in friendship.

*Be a friend.* In order to make a friend, you have to be a friend. You have to be someone that another person would like to have for a friend. There is a whole list of "dos" and "don'ts" involved in being a friend.

# The Dos of Being a Friend

*DO listen.* Don't insist upon being the center of attraction all the time. When your friend speaks, listen to him. A good listener is always popular, not only among young people but among adults too. Everyone likes to talk to someone who listens.

*DO show an interest.* It's important to show an interest in what your friend considers important. You may not be terribly interested in the subject itself, but that does not matter. If you're interested in your friend, you must respect his interests and feelings about what is important to him. Let your friend know that you respect his interests.

*DO be loyal.* If you have something to say that puts your friend in a bad light, say it to him in private — or not at all. Friends should not undermine each other, and friends should not embarrass one another. Loyalty is a very highly prized quality among friends. You never know when you'll need your friend's loyalty.

*DO be open.* When a friend does something that pleases you, be sure he knows it pleases you. Your friend may have done it in the first place in order to make you happy. It is important for him to know that he succeeded. Show your appreciation for gifts, and favors, and visits, and help by thanking him in a way that he knows you mean it. Letting your friend know how you feel about him is always important.

*DO be considerate.* You have to decide how your friends would feel before you do something involving them. If you decide that they would be hurt or angry, you should reconsider doing whatever it is you have in mind.

*DO understand.* Sooner or later, friends disappoint each other in one way or another. Remember that your friend is only human and makes mistakes. But also, try to look at the situation from his point of view, if you can. If you understand *why* your friend did something, even if you thought it was wrong, it will be easier to accept it.

*DO share your feelings, especially about the friendship.* Most kids are embarrassed to tell someone that they like him. This is understandable because telling someone you like him is putting yourself on the line. If your friend tells you some time later that he doesn't like you, you may feel doubly hurt because you have lost face. But usually, telling someone that you like him or enjoy being with him only makes a good friendship better.

*DO give your friends the benefit of the doubt.* Trust is an important part of friendship, and to be a friend you have to trust. If you are hurt or disappointed by your friend once in a while, give him the benefit of the doubt. Assume that he didn't mean to hurt your feelings. Assume that he didn't mean to make you

angry.  Assume that there was a reason that he did
what he did, and try to listen to that reason with an
open mind.

*DO talk over misunderstandings.*  People frequently misunderstand each other.  And many
friendships break up unnecessarily just because nobody talked about a misunderstanding.  If you feel
hurt by something your friend did, speak to him
about it.  Tell him how you feel and ask him to explain.  If a friend comes to you and tells you that you
hurt *him,* consider it a compliment because he wants
to straighten something out and keep the friendship
going.

*DO apologize.*  If you do something that you don't
really mean to do, or if something you do has an
unintentional bad effect on your friend, apologize.
There's nothing wrong with saying, "I'm sorry."  A
lot of things happen by accident, and if you apologize, it is easier for someone to accept the fact that it
really was an accident.

# The Don'ts of Being a Friend

People push other people by acting inconsiderately. These are the don'ts that most commonly break up friendship:

*DON'T talk behind your friend's back.* Whenever you talk behind a friend's back, you're really insulting three persons. You're insulting your friend by discussing him in secret because he cannot defend himself. You're insulting yourself because, by talking behind your friend's back, you are announcing to everyone that you cannot be trusted and that you aren't honest enough to say what you are saying in your friend's presence. And you are insulting the listener because you are telling him that he is the kind of person who would pay attention to gossip.

*DON'T reveal secrets.* If a friend tells you something in secret, keep your word and don't repeat it. And if someone asks, don't even acknowledge that you *know* a secret. If you go around saying "I know something about Jane but I'm not going to tell," it makes others suspicious of Jane, and they may be thinking worse things than if you really did "tell."

People who get a reputation for having a big mouth have trouble winning and keeping friends. If this has happened to you, it's not too late to change or to admit you were wrong. All you have to do is keep your mouth closed.

*DON'T criticize and correct.* No one likes to be criticized by his friends. Every kid has his full share of criticism and correcting from his teachers, his parents, and almost every other adult he comes into contact with. He doesn't need any more from you. If a close friend does something you think is wrong, ask yourself, "Am I the one who should tell him?" Chances are, you're not. If so, keep quiet. Remember that if someone else is going to criticize him for the same thing, he doesn't need your comments. It'll only hurt your friendship.

Of course, if a friend hurts you, then you *are* the one to tell him. You should do it as soon as possible and in private, where no one else can hear you. If your friend hears from someone else that he's mistreating you, then he knows you've been talking behind his back.

*DON'T be a pest.* Remember that even best friends need time to be by themselves. Up to a point, it's fun to call your friends on the telephone and just talk for the fun of talking. But your friend may have homework, or practice, or chores that he must do. Too many calls, or too lengthy calls, may be getting him in trouble at home and he may not feel free enough to tell you.

Also best friends need time to be with other people, including other friends. You may share many interests with your friend, but surely not *all*

interests. Every person is complex and has many
sides. No two people can ever fulfill each other's
needs completely, and friends who try to be everything to each other soon find that it's impossible.
They end up straining the friendship.

*DON'T borrow without returning.* Whenever you
borrow something from a friend, return it at the
time you promised and in at least as good condition
as when you took it. Your friend should not have to
ask for you to return it. Remember when you borrow something from a friend that he considers *valuable,* you're putting your whole friendship in danger
unless you handle it properly. If you break or lose
something your friend considers valuable, he will
feel that you do not care enough for his things, or for
him. He will wonder how much you value his friend-

ship, since you do not value his possessions. Losing or breaking something your friend values only tells him that you don't care very much about his feelings.

Never insist that your friend lend you something he considers valuable. Just because he is unwilling to do so does not mean that he isn't your friend. It usually means that the object you wish to borrow has special meaning to him that only he fully understands. Perhaps his new bike has special meaning to him because it was given to him by his favorite uncle, and his feelings about his uncle are all involved around his feelings about the bike.

Some things, because of their special meaning, are too important to lend to anybody, and you should never insist on borrowing.

*DON'T be moody all the time.* Friends are for sharing feelings — all kinds of feelings, including sad and unpleasant ones. A friend is someone you turn to when things are going badly. Having a friend you can confide in, to tell that you feel hurt, unhappy, or discouraged is very important, but not all the time. Don't overdo it.

No matter how close friends are, no one wants to hear complaints and nagging all the time, even if you have good reason to feel that way. No one likes to be around someone who is always unpleasant to be with. A person who is always complaining, always down in the dumps, always unhappy, is unpleasant to be with. Your friend may sympathize with you a little, but after a while, it will just be boring. Your company will be a drag.

*DON'T brag all the time.* Everybody brags a little. There's nothing wrong with telling a friend about getting a good grade in math after you struggled all year and worried a lot about doing poorly. You did well and you have the right to feel proud of yourself, and it's all right to share such feelings with your friends. But if you overdo it, if you are always saying how wonderful you are at everything, you will push people away from you.

How can you tell if you are bragging too much? It's sometimes difficult to say. If you brag enough so that the people listening to it start to become envious or angry, you are overdoing it. That may seem unfair at times, especially when you have a lot of good news to share, but some people get envious very easily — especially if they feel unsure of themselves. That is the signal, nevertheless. If you have a victory, your friends should feel very good about it for you. If they feel envious, you may be bragging about it too much.

You also have to be very careful about whom you brag *to*. If you are bragging about good school grades to a friend who is doing poorly in school, he may feel you are really telling him that you think you are better than he is. You can see how insulting that can be, and even if you don't mean it, he will be hurt.

Sometimes kids brag, not because they are proud of themselves, but because they are ashamed. They don't feel they are as good as others, and they make up stories to put themselves in a better light. Everyone does this now and then. But almost everyone sees through such "white lies." If you build a whole image for yourself around such bragging, your friends will think less of you and be pushed away. Your friends prefer you the way you really are, or they wouldn't be your friends. Impressing them with excessive bragging will only get you into trouble.

*DON'T be demanding.* Nobody likes to be told

what to do all the time. Kids, especially, hate to be bossed around because they get bossed around so much by adults and because, secretly, they would like to be leaders themselves.

If you start ordering your friends about and making demands on them and insisting that everything be done *your* way, you're going to lose a lot of friends. Other people have rights, too, and part of being a friend is being considerate of those rights.

*DON'T expect perfection.* Don't expect friends to be perfect and never make mistakes. You may want to put your friend on a pedestal because you think so much of him. Some friends like being on a pedestal for a while, but it can get very uncomfortable up there. Your friend will suspect that you are really setting him up for a fall, because he knows he's not that good.

If you expect too much of your friend, he is bound to fall short and disappoint you. And if you go around bragging about your friend — that he can run faster than Billy, for example — you are just setting him up for Billy to beat him. Accept your friends for what they are, not what you would like them to be.

Some kids brag about their friends in order to make themselves sound more important. After all, if Carol is so great, and she's your friend, why you must be pretty good yourself. Most people see through this, and all it does is embarrass Carol.

# Can't Friends Hurt Each Other

Of course they can, and when they do, they often hurt much more than enemies. There's an old saying, "Save me from my friends. I can already protect myself from my enemies." When you get close to a friend, you learn to share your good and bad points, your secrets and your dreams. Friends get to know each other the way they really are, not just the way they appear to others. A friend knows what's really important to you, not just what you tell others is important to you.

When friends fall out, they often hurt each other in the most sensitive way. A friend knows your touchy spots and when he has a fight with you, he might just go for one of those touchy spots . . . and it *hurts*. Why? First, because you feel bad about the

subject to begin with; and second, because your sense of trust is betrayed. Often friends who break up still respect one another's sensitive spots, because they know that their former friend could hurt them back in the same way.

How do you avoid being hurt like that? You can't, really, unless you avoid having friends and that's the worst solution of all. That's what trusting is all about. Sure, some friends will hurt you and there probably isn't a person in the world who hasn't hurt a friend, but friendship is still worth it. A fight in which both friends hurt each other can even serve as an important step in their friendship's growth. If the friends are honest about telling each other how they feel, sometimes the air gets cleared and the friendship continues stronger than ever.

If you have a friendship that is having problems, you should try to sit down with your friend some place where the two of you can be alone and discuss how you both feel about the difficulty. Even if there is no hope of your settling your differences and being friends anymore, you have a good opportunity to learn what it was that went wrong in your friendship, so that you will not make the same mistake in another one.

A friendship is a place where you will grow and learn more about yourself than almost anywhere else.

# ABOUT PUTTING
# YOURSELF DOWN

At one time or another every kid thinks of himself as "inadequate." He thinks he is more stupid than the next fellow, less attractive, and less talented. He thinks he is inferior all around.

There are a lot of reasons why kids feel this way. These feelings are very common, and feeling inadequate some of the time is normal.

Sometimes, however, this "normal" feeling of inadequacy is increased by others who often make kids feel even worse.

Teachers, friends, parents, and other adults sometimes make a kid feel worse about himself than he really needs to.

This chapter will tell you why you sometimes feel down on yourself. It will tell you how others make you feel worse. It will show you what you are doing to yourself. Most of all it will show you how to manage these feelings.

# One of the Reasons You Feel Inadequate . . .

. . . is that if you were compared to most adults, you probably would appear inadequate. What you may not know is that you're *supposed to be* inadequate compared to most adults. That's what growing up is all about.

Adults usually know what they can do well and what they can't do well. Adults generally avoid things they don't do well and concentrate on the things they *can* do well. An adult, doing what he does best, looks like he knows what he's doing. And he should; he's been doing it for years.

Kids, on the other hand, are NOT supposed to know what they can do well. Kids are NOT supposed to know what they like yet. Kids are NOT supposed to concentrate on one or two things they do best and let the others go.

A normal, adequate, healthy kid is on a search — a search for himself. He's supposed to try an activity, a subject in school, a sport, a musical instrument, and then try something else. So long as he keeps looking, he's fine.

But by adult standards, by adult ideas, such a kid is inadequate because he never really perfects anything he does. He's just looking for something he likes.

Unfortunately, most of the standards in this world are adult standards. Young people are constantly being measured against those standards, by adults, by friends, and by themselves. It's really too bad because it gives the wrong impression.

If a kid measures himself with an adult's standards, he almost always comes out looking inferior.

# Nobody Is Good at Everything

Albert Einstein may have been one of the greatest scientists of all time, but he couldn't build a house. Few presidents of the United States were really good baseball players. Some very great doctors were never good at spelling.

The point is that no one is good at everything. And you don't *have* to be good at everything in order to be a success.

Parents, though, expect kids to be good at everything they touch. For some peculiar reason, most parents expect good grades in both math *and* French. Many fathers expect a boy to be *both* musician *and* athlete. Mothers often expect their daughters to be good students *and* good skaters.

Schools generally have the right idea but the

wrong attitude. Kids in school are exposed to many subjects and many different fields, all of which require many different skills. That's good. The trouble comes when the school expects a kid to be good at *all* of them. And the individual teachers have a way of thinking that all the students in *their* class ought to be good at *their* subject. That's ridiculous; it would even be humorous if it didn't make so many students feel so inadequate.

Since nobody is good at everything, but since the adult world often expects this of kids, kids often feel as if they are failures.

It is important to recognize that no adult expects another *adult* to be good at everything. After all, that would be asking too much. Ask any adult.

# But What If You Think You Are Good at Nothing?

Some young people do understand that they don't have to be good at everything. But then they begin to feel that they are good at nothing at all.

When someone says he's not good at anything, he really means that he hasn't found the thing he really likes and can do well. It means he is still looking.

The real advantage to shopping around and looking when you are young is that when you are older, you can make the best decision.

For the fact is, everybody is good at something. It sometimes takes time to find out what it is. That's the whole point about growing up — finding out who you are. Don't worry if you don't know what to do or can't find anything you're good at. Just keep looking.

# Kids Feel Inadequate Because They Lack Experience

When a child is young, he's frequently frightened by the dark, by large animals like elephants, and by powerful natural forces like thunder and lightning.

As he grows older, his experience tells him that elephants are usually friendly, that not much happens in the dark, and that lightning and thunder don't usually hurt him.

In time his fear is replaced by his knowledge that he can cope with these things. He has experience of his own.

A second grade student having trouble with math may feel that he is dumb, different from other kids, and will never learn math. Years later, when he is a sixth grade math student having difficulties, he'll remember he overcame difficulties once before and that he will probably do so again. His experience will help him believe in himself.

An ice skater practicing her first jump and finding it difficult may believe she has no talent and will never become a good skater. By the time she is practicing double jumps, she already knows, from her own experience, that *all* jumps are difficult and that she will succeed in time, if she keeps trying.

That's the way it goes with all experiences. As a person grows older, many of the things that bothered him when he was young disappear. Many of his feelings of inadequacy are replaced with feelings of competence. He has experienced success before and knows, therefore, that difficulties do not automatically mean failure.

It is difficult for a kid to look at himself and say, "The time will come when I won't feel this way." But it's true, and his own experience will help him the most, so long as he keeps trying.

# Kids Often Fail Because They Are Afraid to Fail

When someone has one failure after another, he feels for certain that he is inadequate. A lot of kids don't understand that almost everybody fails at "most" things. Most people are only good at a few. How many people do you know who are physically attractive, get A's in everything, play three musical instruments well (and can sing besides), are great athletes, popular, and get along well with everyone? Most people fail at something.

But when a person is *afraid* to fail, he's more *likely* to fail. Sound silly?

Not really. If a person is afraid to fail, he often

doesn't try as hard. Then, as an excuse, he can say, "The reason I failed was that I really didn't try." Such a failure doesn't hurt his feelings as much as if he really tried and failed.

A student who gets a poor grade on an examination, for example, can try to save face by saying that he didn't study. But if he really did study, if he really did try as hard as he could — and THEN failed — he would feel hurt that much more.

But if you don't really try, you don't find out if you really might have been good or if you might have liked it. If you expect to fail and don't try, you may learn nothing. You may miss out on discovering something important about yourself.

Trying and failing at something is always valuable. If you have tried hard and failed, maybe you should be doing something else. But *not* to have tried and failed doesn't tell you anything at all.

You should approach every activity trying to succeed but keeping in mind that failing is part of learning. Failure hurts, but failure can be useful, too, if you really try.

# Mom and Dad Are Part of the Problem

If your Mom and Dad are like most Moms and Dads, they are part of your problems.

You see, Mom and Dad have "expectations" for you.

Mom's and Dad's expectations often come from their own adult standards. They expect you to do well at school, and they expect a lot of other things of you. They may never say it, but by their reactions to what you do, they make you feel that "success is good, failure is bad." In short, they expect you to succeed. Most children can't live up to their parents' expectations. As a result, they get down on themselves for disappointing their parents. Welcome to the club.

Not only do parents "expect" great things of you, but they may also hope you will fulfill some of the unfulfilled hopes they had for themselves.

If a dad pushes his son to be a great ball player, he may actually be dreaming of his own boyhood when he wished *he* were a great ball player. If a mother wants her daughter to be a doctor, she may really be saying that *she* wanted to be a doctor, but never made it. Parents' expectations are not bad when they are realistic, but if you feel you have to be president to please your parents, you'll probably let them down.

Every child wants his parents to be interested in what he is doing. Every child wants his parents' encouragement and approval. So to some extent, every child has to deal with his parents' unfulfilled dreams. To some degree, what each kid does is influenced by his parents.

There's not much a kid can do about his parents, except to try and understand them. Most parents mean well. Most parents would like their kids to be happy, but they can't help having "expectations."

But it doesn't make you feel any better about yourself when you feel you've let them down.

# Children of Famous Parents Are Especially Unlucky

Some parents are very successful or famous as politicians, authors, or artists. Others have become wealthy or well known in a profession or business.

The children of these parents are especially unlucky. Even if such parents have *no* expectations for their children and try to apply *no* pressures, their own success is a pressure in itself.

If a kid feels he will never succeed like his father no matter what he does, he's bound to feel inadequate. If his parents have "expectations" as well, he is doubly pressured. There may be some advantages to having a rich and successful parent, but there are some distinct disadvantages, too. Such kids feel they have to live up to the family's reputation. They feel they have to get A's just to pass in their family's eyes. They feel they can't be themselves.

It is important to remember that even successful people are usually successful in just one subject. You have to find your own thing to do and be, whether or not it fulfills your family's expectations. After all, when your successful parent broke away from tradition to become a success, he also was finding his own way.

# Teachers Are Part of Your Problem, Too

As a group, teachers can make kids feel dumber faster than almost anyone else. All a teacher has to do is ask a student to answer a question when the teacher *knows* the kid doesn't know the answer. He thereby exposes the kid's inadequacy to the whole class.

A teacher can make a kid feel inadequate even if he does know the answer. When a kid answers correctly, a teacher can act surprised and so indicate to the class that he didn't *expect* the kid to be right. Then everyone knows the teacher thinks the kid's really pretty dumb. Sometimes, you can't win either way.

Why do some teachers do things like that? Surely there must be a better way to teach.

Perhaps such teachers like to show a student up because they themselves feel inadequate. That way, they can prove to everybody listening that at least they are better than the student.

Many teachers, like parents, also have expectations. They expect all kids in their class to be interested in what they have to say. They expect all kids in their class to be interested in *their* subject and good at it, even if they aren't very good teachers.

You already have seen why that's impossible.

In higher grades, some teachers' expectations take the form of threats. "If you don't do well in my subject," they tell their pupils, "you won't be able to go to college," or "you'll be a failure your whole life." Maybe they never say it quite like that, but that's what they mean.

The way to handle a situation like this is to try your best. That *is* part of being a kid. After you've tried your best, you've done your job.

# Other Kids Can Be Very Cruel

Kids can make other kids feel very inadequate.

Kids laugh at other kids when they do something wrong. Kids make fun of other kids for the way they sound, for the way they dress, for the way they think. Kids make fun of other kids sometimes for no reason at all except to make themselves look better by comparison — sound familiar?

That's the way all kids are. You probably do a little showing up of others yourself and for the same reason. It makes you feel better — less inadequate, for the moment anyway.

But here's something you may not know. The kid you would like most to be like also feels inadequate, dumb, ugly, and inferior. The kid who is better than anyone else in math may feel inadequate in art.

The best athlete you know may feel inadequate in French.

Kids who boast about themselves often feel more inadequate than kids who don't boast.

Kids often feel anxious and unsure of themselves. Kids worry about whether they are okay. All kids think they are "different." Kids are unsure about who they are and worry about their futures. Kids worry if their thoughts and feelings are crazy. Kids are troubled by their anger and fear they may lose control.

Since most kids feel this way some of the time, it's likely that you do too. Some kids, usually the ones who won't admit to themselves that they feel inade-

quate, try to make other kids feel bad by pointing out faults in them which they refuse to see in themselves. There's no special way to deal with this, except to try to understand it. If you find some special kid who makes you feel inadequate, who is always telling you what's wrong with you, especially when he has the same problems, just avoid him.

# The Best Way to Deal with Feelings of Inadequacy

The very best way of dealing with feelings of inadequacy is to become good at something so that you learn to respect yourself. That's not the easiest thing to do as you already know.

The first step is to realize that you are yourself, that you are your own person. You have the right to be what you want, to think what you want to think and like what you want to like. It's important to know that everyone wants to please their parents, to have friends, to be popular and to be smart; but it is far more important for you to understand that finding out who you are and what you are really like is the most important thing you will ever do.

The second step is to try. Try again. Try something else. Keep trying.

# ABOUT
# FINDING
# YOURSELF

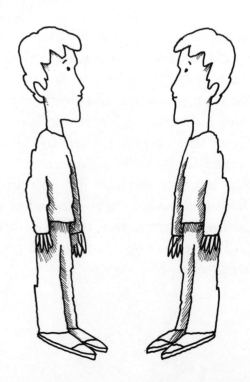

W hen people become good at doing what they like to do, they have found themselves.

Many young people are good at doing things they *do not* like to do. That's not the same thing.

And, of course, many kids would like to do something that they aren't good at.

Also, many kids don't think they're good at anything and don't know what they would like to do.

None of these kids are very happy. And if they don't find something they like and can do well, they won't be very happy adults either.

This chapter is about finding yourself. It tries to help you find out what you really do well and find out what you would really *like* to do. Then it tries to see if there is some way to get those two ideas together.

But a word of warning. Finding yourself, especially when you are young, is not a one-time thing. You can find yourself now and be lost a year from now because your interests have changed. It's a good idea to keep checking to see if your interests *have* changed.

# Why It Is Difficult to Find Yourself

It shouldn't be difficult to find what you like and can do well — but for most kids, and most adults too, it is. There are a lot of different influences.

Pleasing parents is very important to all kids. But some kids end up working to be someone their *parents* would like, instead of working to become someone they *themselves* could like.

Others seem to like only what their parents dislike. Such kids are still reacting to their parents, but in a negative way. They automatically reject many things they may be secretly pleased with, just because they don't want to appear to please their parents.

Schools try to encourage students in ways that please the school. A school's goals may have very little to do with what is important to a kid or what he may be good at.

Groups of friends often set standards of what is good and what is bad, what you should like and what you shouldn't. These standards may also send you off in a wrong direction. You can be meeting all the group's standards and still not be helping yourself.

Also, our whole society, our culture, rewards certain kinds of success and not others. People pay a lot of money for one kind of skill and very little for another. It doesn't mean that the lower paying skill may not be the better one for a particular person. People who take up a career for money are never as happy as people who do something because they love it.

# Try It: You May Like It

It is impossible to decide whether or not you like something until you have tried it. It sounds obvious, but many people do not think trying something new is necessary. It is.

Give each idea a *fair* trial — not a brief brush. If you have decided to try out something new, also decide how long you will stick with it before you can make a fair judgment. For example, if you decide that you would like to play the violin, you should plan to take more than one lesson before you can know anything about your potential skill or interest.

Then, the best thing to judge is not the goal but the process of reaching the goal. Almost everybody

would like to be highly skilled. But becoming highly skilled at anything requires a great deal of time and work. You must decide if you enjoy working toward the goal.

It's not enough to want to be a great violinist. You also have to like the process of becoming a great violinist. Do you enjoy the lessons? Do you enjoy practicing? If you would enjoy being a great violinist but hate the work, forget it. Being a great violinist means loving the work involved in becoming one.

It's a good plan to try as many ideas as possible when you are still young. That's the time for self-discovery. Don't restrict yourself to the few goals and standards that other people think you should try. Expand your views as far as you can.

## Be Prepared to Fail

Finding yourself means not only that you find out what you're good at and what you like, it also means discovering what you're *not* good at and what you *don't* like. Knowing what isn't right for you is almost as valuable as knowing what is. Both help to steer you in the right direction.

Everyone gets upset when he fails at something,

but that can be valuable. Although most kids would be upset if they found that they had failed an advanced math course, they have actually learned a great deal about themselves. They know they should not become engineers or physical scientists and that they would not be good at accounting work or work that involves statistics. So failing could help a kid to lead a much happier life if he drew the right conclusion from the failing: that he isn't so much a failure as unsuited to the particular subject.

# What Makes You Happy?

Now for the details of helping you find yourself.

Get a piece of paper and a pencil. This next part must be done in writing, so that you can look at it later. Take some time to think about your answers, and then write them down clearly.

Prepare a list of your happiest memories. Put them down in the order that they occur to you. And put down what you *really* found to be your happiest memories — not the ones you think you *should* put down.

A sample list might look like this:

1. The time I went camping for a weekend.
2. The time I was named to the town all-star team.
3. The time I was applauded for my piano recital.
4. The time I went back to my old school and everyone remembered me.
5. The time I spend with Franz, my dog.
6. When I got great grades on my report card.

The list can be as long as you like, but most lists will contain between six and ten items. Remember, these are not just "happy" times but the *happiest* ones.

When you have finished this list, go right on to the next one. You will come back to look at it later.

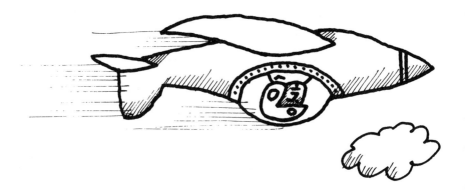

# Make Three Wishes

On another piece of paper — again do this in writing — make three wishes. Any kind of wishes. Take some time to think about them, and then write them down. But be sure to write *your* wishes, not someone else's wishes for you.

A sample list of wishes:

1. I wish I were an airplane pilot.

2. I wish my father would spend more time with me.

3. I wish I were the most popular kid in school.

If you really want to wish for four or five things, it's okay, but be sure you put your wishes down in the same order you thought of them. Then, put the list aside with the other one.

# List Five People Whom You Really Admire

The people can be anybody. Your parents. The President of the United States. The math teacher Your neighbor or your friend. Anybody at all.

Next to each name, write down *why* you admire him. "Really smart" might be one reason; "good looking" might be another; "very rich" might be a third reason.

Then add the list to the pile of others and get ready for making out another one.


# Make a List of Unpleasant Memories

Make this list as long as you like, but include at *least* five items. Think. Everybody has at least five unpleasant memories. Put them down in the order that they occur to you.

One's kid's list might be:

1. The time I flunked French when I really thought I did well.

2. The time I struck out with the bases loaded in the championship game.

3. The time my mother made me cut my hair.

4. The time I was sick and thought I was dying.

5. The time I goofed in English class and everybody laughed.

Put the list aside. There is only one more to make.


# List Five Compliments That People Have Paid You

Everybody has had compliments — from friends, parents, teachers. Think back and list five compliments that you have received and who gave them to you. Put them down in the order that they occur to you, just as with the other lists. Especially put down compliments that you have heard from more than one person or more than one time.

One kid's "compliments" list might be:

1. The day I learned to ski parallel and my instructor applauded.

2. The day the teacher called me a "real brain."

3. The time I sang the lead in the school musical and everybody said it was great.

4. The time I fixed dinner and mother said I was a good cook.

5. The time Billy said I was the best dancer he ever saw.

# Go Back to All Five Lists

Spread out all five lists on a table before you. You will see that everything you have written, line by line, will fall into one of several categories, such as:

*Personal:* Achievement of any kind is considered personal.

*Social:* Anything related to popularity, acceptance by others, is considered social.

*Family:* Anything related to brother, sisters, parents are at least part family.

*Material:* All items related to possessions or money are considered material.

List the category in parentheses next to the line.

For example:

"I wish I were an airplane pilot." (Personal)

If you wrote "I wish I were an airplane pilot because they make a lot of money," it would be considered Personal *and* Material.

"I wish my father would spend more time with me." (Family)

When you have listed one or more categories next to every line you have written on all five lists, you will be ready to evaluate your comments.

# How to Analyze the Categories

First, look at all five lists and see if there is one category that appears on the lists more than others. You may discover that all your wishes, admirations, compliments, and unpleasant memories are related to the personal category. This indicates that you should try to find yourself by setting some tasks which you can accomplish by yourself. You are the sort of person who is happiest achieving something for yourself.

If the social category appears often, you should be involved in relationships with other people: your peer group, your school friends, and so forth.

If your answers fall into the family category a good part of the time, it means that you've been happiest and received the most fulfilling rewards within your own family and that working with or in a family may be especially satisfying to you.

If the material category appears frequently, you are interested in making money and having the possessions money can buy. It's okay to want material possessions, but when acquiring possessions becomes your major goal, it's better to find out more about yourself.

Fortunately, most kids' lists will have a mixture of all four categories. No one is motivated totally by only one set of values, but it's a good idea to know in which direction you're leaning. It may help you decide later on.

## What the Lists Really Represent

The HAPPIEST MEMORY list is a guide to what you'd really like to do and what gives you the most satisfaction. The order in which you put your items down suggests how important you think the items are, EXCEPT you may find something really important, as you think it over, pretty far down the list. You may have been cautious about admitting something that made you happy, probably because you thought there was something wrong with it.

The PEOPLE MOST ADMIRED list contains the names of people you really, deep down, would most like to be like. See how many of them have accomplishments in the same categories as your HAPPIEST MEMORY lists.

The THREE WISHES list contains the items you *think* will make you happy. They should relate pretty well to your HAPPIEST MEMORY list. If they don't seem to have any connection at all, you're probably being too unrealistic and you could be very, very difficult to satisfy. You may be supposing that something you have little experience with will make you happy, and that rarely works.

The UNPLEASANT MEMORY list tells where you are most vulnerable, how you are most easily hurt. This, too, should agree, at least in categories, with your HAPPIEST MEMORY list. Generally people can't be hurt in situations they don't care about.

The COMPLIMENTS list is ordinarily a guide to what other people think you do well, but in this case it is also a guide to what *you* think you do well. If you received compliments on your singing, but knew you weren't that much of a singer, you wouldn't have put it on the list.

# What to Do About All This?

There is no magical formula to finding yourself. You do not take the lists and multiply by three to get an answer.

But if you study your lists, you should have a pretty good idea of what pleases you, what hurts you, what other people think, and perhaps what you are pretty good at.

Try exploring new ideas and don't worry about failing. The ideas you should try first are the ones that are in areas similar to those on your "happiest memory" list and the ones you have received compliments on.

If you study the lists, you should have a pretty good picture of yourself. Being happy and doing something you like and are good at depends upon your finding something that suits your personality and natural abilities.

Most important, don't allow yourself to be trapped by one fixed point of view about yourself when you are young. Keep these lists in a safe place. Do the lists again next year, and compare. Try them on your friends. Discuss them with your parents. They should and will change each year and so will your understanding of what the lists mean.

Once you've looked over all the lists, try to find something that fits into the category you seem to like most. It may not be perfect, but it's the best place to start. And everything begins as a small step.

# ABOUT
# PARENTS'
# DIVORCE

$\text{A}$ lot of kids worry about their parents' divorce. Much needless worry could be done away with if kids had more information. Here is some information.

1. Nobody is divorcing you. Your father and mother divorce each other, but neither one divorces you. Neither parent is rejecting you.

2. After their divorce your mother will still be your mother, and your father will still be your father. And they always will be.

3. You probably will not have to go to court, speak to any judges or lawyers, or anything like that.

4. You have no choice in your parents' divorce. You have no decisions to make. You have no vote. Although you are affected by it, it's your parents' business.

5. THE DIVORCE IS NOT YOUR FAULT. You may think the divorce is happening because of something you

did or didn't do, or because you were bad, or because you wished it to happen. This just isn't true. THE DIVORCE IS ABSOLUTELY NOT YOUR FAULT.

6. Probably you will live with your mother and she will take care of you. You will probably live in the same house, go to the same school, and have the same friends as you do right now.

7. No matter what happens, someone will still take care of you. You will not be abandoned to yourself.

Before you go on, reread this list again. And try to believe it. Many kids' worries about a divorce can be helped by understanding these points.


# Why Your Parents Are Getting Divorced

One of the ways to understand why people get divorced is to understand some of the reasons people get married in the first place. Two people may get married because they think they love each other and think they will always love each other. People get married because they think they want to spend the rest of their lives together. Some people get married because they have special needs of their own, and they think their partner will be able to fulfill these needs. And people get married because they think they will be happy together.

There's a lot of "thinking" in those statements, and sometimes things don't work out the way people think. People grow. People change. Sometimes they grow and change in different ways until they have very little in common with each other. And much of the "thinking" they had done years ago may no longer be true. Sometimes people just make mistakes; they misjudged their partner years ago or misjudged themselves.

When married people find out that they made a mistake about each other, that they do not (or no longer) love each other, or that the partner does not (or no longer) fulfills their needs, they get very unhappy. Usually it's nobody's fault, though each person in a divorce often blames the other.

When married people become very unhappy with each other, they have a choice between staying married and unhappy, or getting divorced. Often, even though they know it will hurt the kids and they are sorry about that, they decide they must get a divorce.

There are millions of divorced people in this country. About one in three marriages end up in divorce. There are millions of children whose parents are divorced. You are certainly not alone.

# How Kids Feel About Their Parents' Divorce

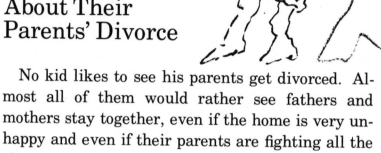

No kid likes to see his parents get divorced. Almost all of them would rather see fathers and mothers stay together, even if the home is very unhappy and even if their parents are fighting all the time.

So when a kid hears that his parents are divorcing each other, *he feels anxious and afraid.* He is worried about what will happen to him, who will take care of him, whether he will have to move, whether his friends will still like him, and how he will get along without his father. Sometimes he appears anxious over silly things — will he still be able to go to the movies next weekend — but deep down he is anxious about very real fears.

*He feels angry.* He feels angry at his mother, angry at his father, and frequently angry at himself. He is about to lose something very important to him, and even if he understands why the divorce is taking place, the loss is still important. Losses of important things lead to deep hurts, and deep hurts lead to much anger.

*He feels guilty.* Even if his parents have told him differently, he may still feel the divorce is somehow his fault. Or, at the very least, he may still feel that there is something he could have done to change things. He cannot believe that the divorce is happening and affecting his life in such a major way but really has nothing to do with him. Sometimes his anger about the divorce is so great, he feels guilty about that.

*He feels sad.* Right after a divorce, a kid often misses his father very much and misses all the things they used to do together. He often gets very sad and loses interest in eating, schoolwork, friends, and so forth. All these feelings are not only natural and normal, they are expected.

The best way to relieve your fears is to find out the truth. Ask about anything you want to know. The best way to deal with the anger is to express it — talk to someone about it. The best way to deal with the guilt is to believe that kids are never the cause of a divorce. And talk about your feelings with someone who will understand. The best way to deal with the sadness is to give it time. Time will heal the wounds and, sooner or later, the sadness will go away. The worst thing you can do is to walk around feeling sorry for yourself.

# The Secret Hope of Every Kid of Divorced Parents

Every kid whose parents are divorced secretly hopes that his parents will marry each other again.

He may have been told a hundred times by his mother and by his father that such hopes are impossible, but that usually does not stop a kid from hoping. This is especially true right after the divorce.

The marriage itself may have been a very bad one, with fighting and arguments all the time, but that doesn't seem to matter to the kid. He wants his parents married.

Often, kids make elaborate plans to get their parents together again.

Sometimes they invent illness. Sometimes they tell each parent stories about the other that they feel will help. Sometimes they decide that if they are very, very good from now on, maybe their fathers will come back and live with them. Sometimes they plead with their mothers and fathers, directly asking them to remarry.

This can be very, very uncomfortable for the divorced parents. Both father and mother feel more guilty than ever about their divorce, knowing how much it has hurt the kids. But usually they remember that they divorced for good reason and that staying together was too painful for them to remarry. In any case, very few divorced people ever marry each other again. If a kid keeps to this secret hope, he will remain sad and angry and feel guilty for a long, long time.

However painful it is, a kid has to accept the divorce as a fact of life. He cannot, and should not, spend his emotions on the empty hope that it was all a bad dream and that, somehow, he can get them together again.

# What One Divorced Parent Says About the Other

You should not look to your mother for accurate information about your father — and you should not look to your father for accurate information about your mother — after they are divorced.

Why?

Because one divorced parent is a very poor judge of the other, and the information each gives a kid about the other is often wrong.

A mother, for example, may tell a kid that the father is no good, that the divorce was all his fault, and that the father no longer, and possibly never

did, love his kids. Many fathers say the same things about a kid's mother.

Another mother, in an effort to be very "fair," may say nothing bad about a kid's father. She may make him out to be a saint, believing that in that way she is protecting her children. Many fathers do the same thing.

Both approaches are wrong. Most mothers and fathers are both good and bad. They are all certainly human, with all the virtues and faults that being human means.

The best thing to do is make your own judgments, even though you may still be young. Your interpretation will be better than either of your parents' after they are divorced.

## Some of the Problems of Dealing with a Divorced Mother

Living with your divorced mother may cause some special problems. You can probably handle them better if you know about them.

*Your mother will probably work.* She works because she needs the money for herself and for you — not because she doesn't love you. Many mothers who are not divorced also work. It is not a good idea to make it difficult for your mother to hold a job by making a big fuss over it. You'd only be hurting yourself.

*Your mother may be dating.* Many kids get upset when their mothers begin to date other men. They sometimes become upset because they have decided they wouldn't like the man to be their stepfather, often long before their mothers have even thought about such things. If your mother dates several men, and you think about each as a possible stepfather all the time, you can see how confused you can become. Your mother dates because she needs some adult fun now and then, just as you need fun. You will get along better with your mother if you understand and accept this.

*Your mother may want you to grow up too quickly.* Divorced mothers are often lonely and sometimes share adult problems with their kids. Sometimes this can be very hard. For example, most money problems, or problems with your father, or dating problems are really adult problems that your mother should handle herself. If she tries to involve you, the best thing for you to say is "I can't deal with that," and try to get her to change the subject. On the other hand, you may be expected to help her more often with the shopping or the cleaning, or things like that. You should be willing to cooperate on such problems, even if you didn't have to before.

*Your mother may want you to stay a baby.* Some mothers, after divorce, act as if they don't want their kids to grow up at all. For example, if you are old enough to know how much to eat, how warmly you should dress, and so forth, and you were making those decisions before the divorce, don't let your mother start making those decisions for you. Kids of divorced parents have the right to grow up just like any other kids, and you may have to remind your mother now and then not to treat you as a baby. And you may have to fight your own feelings because it's very tempting to allow your mother to do everything for you.

*Your mother may be getting married again.* As time goes by, your mother may decide to marry again. Most kids approve of this idea. They think it would be nice to have a man around the house. But also, many kids worry about not being liked by the new husband, and worry about how their life will be changed, and worry about whether their mother will love them as much now that she loves another person, too. Although it's not usual for a mother to ask her kid's permission to marry, most mothers do not suddenly spring such events on their kids. Your mother will probably give you some time to get used to the idea of her marrying again. And she would not consider marrying anybody who would not like you. But most important, just because she loves someone else *doesn't mean she loves you less.* Love doesn't work like that.

# Some of the Problems of Dealing with a Divorced Father

Most kids of divorced parents live with their mothers and either visit their fathers from time to time or have their fathers visit them. This relationship raises some problems which you can also probably manage if you know something about them in advance.

*Good guy father.* Many fathers, because they only

see their kids once in a while, buy them fancy presents, take them to interesting, fun places, and never scold them. Because they seldom visit, some fathers think they have to show their kid a good time. There are two things wrong with this. First, compared to the everyday routines that you must go through with your mother, your father looks like the "good guy." That's not true and that's not fair to your mother.

Second, such frantic activity can be exhausting. Most kids just want to be with their fathers, not at the ball park or at the circus — just *with them*. It is all right to tell your father that you'd love to see him and do "nothing" — just hang around and maybe talk. It's not just all right, it's important.

*Some fathers don't visit.* Occasionally, a father doesn't take advantage of his visiting rights. He might have to take care of business out of town, or he might be very busy. If this happens to you, you should talk to him and ask him whether he likes to visit with you or not. Tell him that you expect him and that you are counting on his visits, and if he can't make one, he should tell you in advance and set up another time. If your father never visits, you should probably try to stop thinking about him. There's something wrong with a person like that. It's not your fault, even though it hurts. If your father moves to another part of the country, you should make arrangements through your mother to see him on school vacations and holidays.

*Some fathers take brothers and sisters out together.* This is okay some of the time, but not always. You have the right to spend some time with your father all by yourself now and then. And if you have brothers and sisters, they have the same rights, too. You should talk to your father and tell him that you would like some time with him alone, and that he should make such arrangements.

*Some fathers undermine mothers.* If you are living with your mother, your mother is the boss. It is her responsibility to raise you. Sometimes, fathers who visit occasionally defeat that effort. For example, if you had a bad report card and your mother is making you study one hour more a day, your father may tell you that you don't have to do that. This is really unfair of your father and can get you very confused. If you live with your mother, and your father and mother tell you opposite things, you have to follow what your mother says.

*Disagreeing with your father about what to do.* Sometimes, fathers who are visiting their kids want to do things that the kid hates. Sometimes, the kid wants to do something that the father hates. It is usually best to avoid either of those things and end up doing something both father and kid can enjoy.

Once in a great while it is all right for one or the

other to give in, just to make the other one happy. But it is a mistake to do it very often.

*Not wanting to see your father.* Some kids think that they *have* to visit with their fathers whether they want to or not. This is not really so. You have to see your father some of the time, but you do not have to see him all the time that you are permitted to see him. If you have an important game or just don't feel like seeing him one week, it is all right to tell him so. Call him up in advance so that he isn't waiting for you. Just because your parents got divorced doesn't mean your whole life has to be upset by it.

*Your father may be getting married again.* Sometimes fathers remarry before or after mothers do. Your father is still your father. Even if he marries somebody who has kids of her own, he is still your father. He will probably continue to visit you the same way he always has. The big difference is that now you will have a special place to go to visit him — his new home with his new wife, and maybe his new family. It is also important to realize that just because he loves someone else it doesn't mean he loves you *less*.

Chances are that if your father remarries, many of the other problems talked about in this section will go away because he will treat you more like a member of a family than someone special to visit.

# Getting Caught in the Middle

Remember, if your parents get divorced they are very upset with each other, and they might be doing a lot of things they wouldn't do if they could look at it calmly. Possibly, they might try to use you to get back at each other.

For example, there are some divorced parents who communicate with each other through the kid. The mother says, "Tell your father that . . ." or the father says, "Tell your mother that I think . . ." If you hear a sentence beginning with such words, ask your parents to talk to each other directly. Don't become their message carrier.

Some divorced parents pump their kids for information about the other one. Your father might ask you whether your mother is dating, or ask what she is doing about this or that. Mothers do the same. They ask a kid who has returned from a visit to the father all about what his new life is like. You should not get involved in things like that. If your father wants to know what your mother is doing, he should ask your mother directly. And if your mother wants to know about your father, she should ask him too. Many kids, trying to please everybody,

end up as secret agents, carrying tales, for both sides. This is not a good idea. Some divorced parents try to get their kid to side with them against the other. Your mother might paint a picture of your father in such a way as to get you to agree with

her against him. Don't take sides. Don't become an ally of your father against your mother, or an ally of your mother against your father. You already know that their opinions of each other are likely to be mistaken.

# The Really Important Things to Remember

Your parents did not divorce because of you.

Kids are often better off living with a divorced parent than living in a house with two people who do not want to stay married.

Even if you decide that your mother or father doesn't love you (in rare cases, it may be true), that does not mean there is anything wrong with you, and it does not mean you are not lovable to someone else.

You are not alone. There are millions of other kids in this country who also live with divorced parents, and they come out okay.

If you feel terribly unhappy, the best thing to do is to talk to someone about it.